SOARING

Written by DAN HALACY
Photographed by JAMES TALLON

J.B. LIPPINCOTT COMPANY

Philadelphia and New York

U.S. Library of Congress Cataloging in Publication Data

Halacy, Daniel Stephen, birth date
  Soaring.

  SUMMARY: Describes the aircraft and the techniques used in "sailing" the air.
  1. Gliding and soaring. [1. Gliding] I. Tallon, James, illus. II. Title.
TL765.H34   797.5'5   72-2319
ISBN-0-397-31248-2   ISBN-0-397-31322-5 (lib. bdg.)

Text copyright © 1972 by D. S. Halacy, Jr.
Photographs copyright © 1972 by James Tallon
All rights reserved
Printed in the United States of America
First Edition

Soaring—powerless flight in a craft called a glider or a sailplane—is one of the most exciting of sports. Thousands of pilots, some of them as young as fourteen, ride the sky on near-silent wings to climb "where never lark or even eagle flew," remaining aloft for hours at a time and sometimes covering hundreds of miles on a single flight.

Man soared long before he flew in powered aircraft, and the Wright brothers set a glider record for endurance some sixty years ago. Today, soaring combines the thrills of flight with the fun of the outdoors and fellowship with other enthusiasts.

The young man or woman learning to soar does not step right into a sleek, high-performance sailplane, of course. Training begins in two-place training gliders, generally of high-wing design and rugged construction.

Except for the lack of an engine, a sailplane is very similar to an airplane and the same rules of safety apply. Soaring craft can be disassembled for storage or for carrying on a trailer. Assembly must be carefully done before the craft is ready for flight.

Lacking its own power to climb, the glider must be gotten aloft in some other manner. Sometimes an automobile is used to tow the glider into the air; sometimes an engine-powered winch does the job. But towing by airplane is the most used method.

The towrope is attached to a hook under the fuselage. A handle inside the cockpit releases the rope when sufficient altitude has been reached. A ground-crew member attaches the towrope and the pilot checks the release action.

When the sailplane pilot is ready for takeoff, the towplane pilot takes up slack in the towline and then moves his rudder back and forth. The sailplane pilot answers with a similar signal and the towplane begins to roll.

Flying behind the towplane is one of the most difficult parts of flight training and is excellent practice for the would-be pilot. When flown properly the sailplane remains directly behind the towplane and slightly above. Generally the sailplane pilot tries to keep the towplane on the horizon.

When sufficiently high—usually about 2,000 feet above the ground—the sailplane is released from the towrope. Training flights are generally quite short at first and often just a slow glide back to the runway.

After about twenty to thirty flights the student can fly on tow, maneuver his craft in the air, and carry out his landing approach and touchdown. He may also have learned some basic "thermal" flying techniques that enable him to soar rather than just glide downhill. Now he is ready to solo. Many young pilots achieve this thrill at age fourteen.

With his basic lessons learned, the pilot is now ready to master more advanced techniques and begin enjoying the thrills of powerless flight. This may involve training in a higher performance craft.

Gravity furnishes the power for gliders and sailplanes. Some craft can attain speeds that exceed 150 miles an hour. Because of their fine streamlining some sailplanes can glide more than forty feet forward for every foot they come down. Drag parachutes are often used to make landing easier.

Soaring is flying a sailplane in rising air. There are three kinds of soaring: "thermaling" in rising bubbles or columns of warm air; ridge soaring in the wind rushing up a mountainside; and "wave soaring" downwind of mountains under certain meteorological conditions.

To help him find lift, the soaring pilot relies on a "variometer," which is a very sensitive and fast-acting altimeter. When the variometer needle indicates lift, the pilot flies his craft so as to stay in the rising air. The variometer is also helpful in locating sinking air—from which the pilot tries to escape as quickly as possible!

Surest indication of rising currents are those puffy cumulus clouds we are all familiar with. Updrafts as strong as 2,000 feet per minute and more have been encountered by soaring pilots and ridden to great heights. Violent rising currents exist inside thunderclouds and wise pilots have learned to avoid these.

Often there will be more than one sailplane in a good thermal. Here the safety rule dictates that all circle in the same direction, to guard against collision.

On days when the sky is cloudless there may still be thermals. These "dry" thermals have been used for many long flights. Often they are marked by dust devils but sometimes soaring pilots must trust to their variometers—and a little luck.

Ridge soaring was first done by pioneer glider pilots decades ago in the Wasserkuppe in Germany. Today there are many places where sailplanes can fly for hours on the strong ridge lift as wind blows over mountains or cliffs.

All turns made in ridge soaring are away from the ridge, and care must be taken not to fly over the crest of the ridge since strong downdrafts may be encountered on the lee side. This kind of soaring is great sport but calls for constant vigilance.

A challenging kind of flying is "wave soaring." A relatively rare phenomenon occurring in only certain localities, a wave has carried a sailplane as high as 46,000 feet, which is a world record. The pilot must cope with strong winds and perhaps severe turbulence. He must also carry along oxygen for breathing at high altitudes.

Wave formations are typically marked by "lenticular" or lens-shaped clouds. Often these are stacked one above the other and secondary wave clouds may form downwind of the first. Properly located in the wave lift, a pilot is treated to a surprisingly smooth and powerful climb.

Once a pilot has mastered thermaling techniques and perhaps flown in ridge or wave lift, he begins to think of flying cross-country. This takes some courage, getting away from the safety of his home airport. Once over this mental hurdle he is ready for the sheer sport of riding the thermals and the wind to a predetermined goal, and sometimes back home again.

Navigation is important to the sailplane pilot. A cross-country flight may be planned downwind for as much distance as possible. It may be a "speed triangle," rounding two distant turn points and returning to the takeoff point. Or it may be an "out-and-return" of hundreds of miles. Pictures must be taken to prove the sailplane flew over the turn point.

In addition to a good sailplane the pilot will need a radio, and sometimes a retrieve crew. Pulling a trailer, and in constant contact with the pilot, such a crew is a great confidence builder and saves time in the event of an off-field landing.

Each year there are many local and regional contests, and several national competitions. The goal of the serious contest pilot is to be selected for international competition. Sailplanes of less than 50-foot wingspan are "Standard" class; those larger than this compete in "Open" class contests.

A pilots' meeting is held before each contest day. Besides being told what their task will be, the pilots are briefed on best routes, safety precautions, and the very important element of weather.

The world distance record is held jointly by two American pilots who flew 717 miles in similar craft. The altitude mark is also held by an American: 46,000 feet over the Sierras in California. Speed records continue to climb and a South African pilot has averaged more than 94 miles an hour around a 100-kilometer course.

Achievement badges given by the Soaring Society of America make soaring more interesting. The highest award is the Diamond, requiring a distance flight of 500 kilometers (312 miles); flight to a predetermined goal of 300 kilometers (192 miles); and an altitude gain of 5,000 meters (16,000 feet) above release point. All such flights must be carefully documented, either by witnesses or photographs and barograph tracings.

A high-performance sailplane is not just an excellent aircraft but a beautiful work of art as well. Fiber glass is the material favored for most of these craft, giving strength and incredible smoothness. Flying such sleek sailplanes is the goal of most pilots.

But even the student pilot, circling in his first thermal, knows something of the thrills of soaring flight.